Bluebirds
and Blessings

By Jennifer Robin

Illustrations by A. Shelton

Copyright 2013 Jennifer Robin

Illustrations by A. Shelton
Used by permission

ISBN 978-1-937975-14-2

For His Glory
An imprint of RNWC Media

RNWC Media LLC
PO Box 559
Pinehurst TX 77362

www.RNWCMedia.com

God came to me in a dream one night
  to teach me a lesson, a lesson about life.

Blessings will come to rest in your hand.

I opened my palm and a bird came to stand.

He was brilliant, blue, delicate and cheerful.

My heart welled up over a bird so joyful.

Singing softly and sweetly, each note on key.

Quite the composer and performer was he!

Worshiping the God of Creation,
  chirping out notes with no hesitation.

The bird rested after his song,
 thinking, I'm sure, about moving on.

I could not lose this amazing gift!

So I closed my hand, tightly clenching my fist.

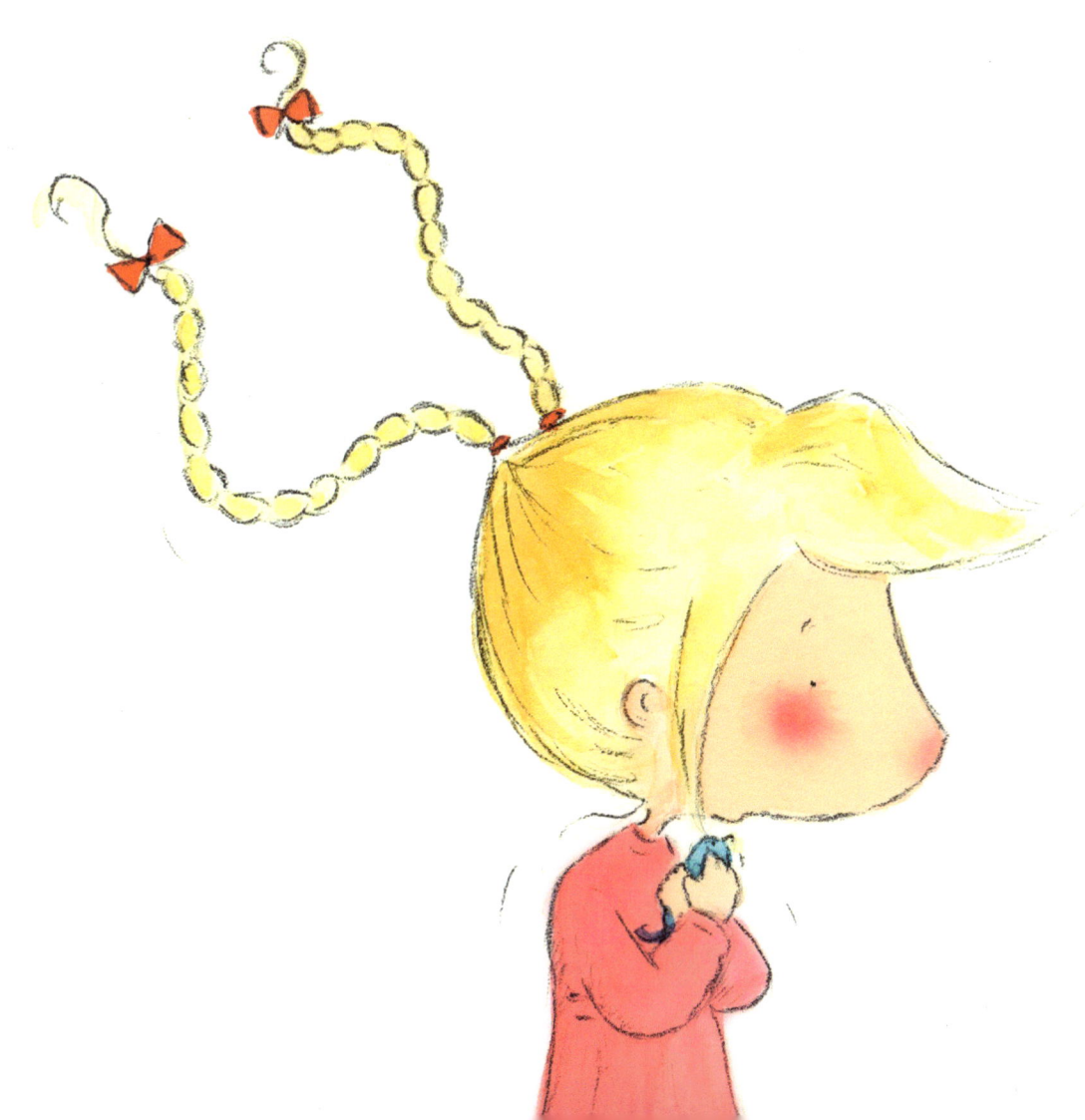

Feelings of fear crept into me,
 the fear of my new friend flying free.

Would he stay or would he go?
Who can survive in a hand so closed?

Unwillingly, I loosened my grip.
Immediately that bird did flit.

Off to a branch way up high
   to breathe the fresh air of a cloudless sky.

I sat and cried, "What am I to do?"

Whatever happened to my bird so blue?

But God's creatures are meant to live freely

where palms are stretched open
and friendships are easy.

God wants to fill you with blessings so grand

if you'll open your heart, not just your hand.

www.ingramcontent.com/pod-product-compliance
Lightning Source LLC
Chambersburg PA
CBHW041122070526
44584CB00002B/251